The Quotable Anaïs Nin

THE QUOTABLE ANAÏS NIN

365 Quotations with Citations

Collected and compiled by
Paul Herron

With engravings by Ian Hugo

SKY BLUE PRESS
San Antonio, Texas

Published by Sky Blue Press, San Antonio, Texas

ISBN: 978-0-9889170-6-4

Library of Congress Control Number: 2015954907

eBook ISBN: 978-0-9889170-4-0

Special thanks to:

Sara Herron

The Anaïs Nin Trust

Tree and Devon Wright

Kim Krizan

Chip Mosher

PRINTS BY IAN HUGO ARE AS FOLLOWS:

PHOTOGRAPHS ARE AS FOLLOWS:

TABLE OF CONTENTS

INTRODUCTION

Besides her famous diaries and erotica, Anaïs Nin (1903-1977) is known for her inspirational and insightful quotations. When one googles "Anaïs Nin quotes," more than 480,000 websites appear, making her one of the most oft-quoted authors on the web. This alone is reason enough to collect her most popular and meaningful quotations into one book, but there is another as well: the inaccuracies and misinformation which frequently occur in our cut-and-paste internet culture.

The Quotable Anaïs Nin rectifies these errors by taking each quotation word for word directly from its source and accurately citing it. If a quotation found on the web does not exist in Nin's work, it is not included here, which means some popular sayings attributed to Nin are absent. Examples of this include the poem "Risk," which begins with "And the day came when the risk to remain tight in a bud…" and "Good things happen to those who hustle." Not only do these quotations not belong to Nin, evidence suggests that the true authors are Elizabeth Appell and Chuck Noll, respectively. There are probably dozens of other misattributed "Nin quotes" floating around the web.

The contents of *The Quotable Anaïs Nin* are divided into general themes that reflect the characteristics of Nin's writing: lust for life, love and sensuality, consciousness, women and men, and writing and art. Within each category, the quotations are arranged and numbered according to the title of their sources. Quotations from Nin's unpublished diaries are cited as "unpublished diary, 1948," etc. The novels included in *Cities of the Interior* are cited using the pagination from the collection, not the individually published novels.

When quotations appear in more than one source, the following protocol is used: the quote from the earliest source is used unless the wording in a newer source is more widely known. For example, in the original handwritten diary of the 1940s, Nin wrote, "Life shrinks in proportion to one's courage," which appears in *Mirages: The Unexpurgated Diary of Anaïs Nin*, 1939-1947 (published in 2013). During the editing process for the third volume of *The Diary of Anaïs Nin* (published in 1969), Nin changed the wording to "Life shrinks or expands in proportion to one's courage," which is the most recognizable version and, therefore, the one used here.

The Quotable Anaïs Nin is not only a useful reference book, it is also a source of thought-provoking and stimulating quotations, one for each day of the year. The fact that this book is digitally searchable will surely enhance its value to readers and scholars alike.

Each quotation can be considered a stone in a broader, more comprehensive mosaic which gives it a deeper meaning. It is my hope that the quotations will inspire readers to explore the context in which they appear in Anaïs Nin's books.

—*Paul Herron*, October, 2015

I never ate before, in this deep carnal way... I have only three desires now: to sleep, to eat, and to fuck. The cabarets excite me. I want to hear their hoarse music, to see faces, to brush against bodies, to drink fiery Benedictine. Beautiful women arouse fierce desires in me. Handsome men. Pawing. I want drugs. I want perverse people — to know them, be intimate with them. I never look at naive faces. Oh, god, I feel now the full urge to depravation which I felt with June. I want to bite into life, and to be torn by it. I want hotel rooms, that hour of voluptuousness without thought and without feeling. Henry does not give me this... I have aroused his love. Curse his love. He can fuck me as no one else can — but I want more than that. I'm going to hell... to hell, to hell. Wild. wild. wild.

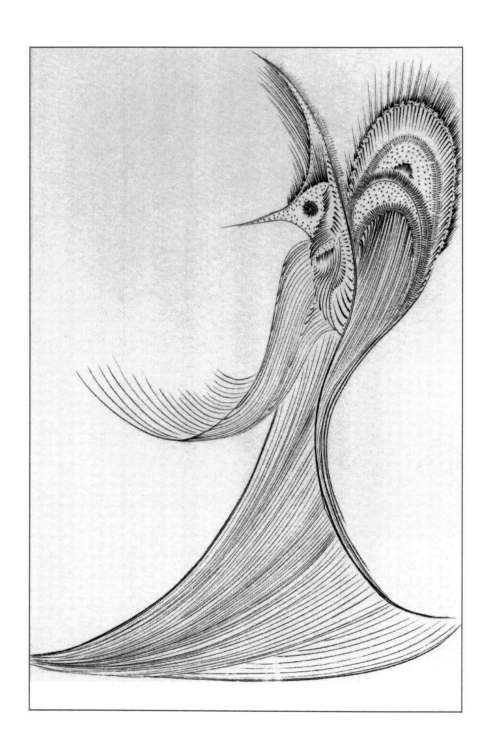

LUST FOR LIFE

· 1 ·

I must be a mermaid... I have no fear of depths and a great fear of shallow living.

—The Four-Chambered Heart, in Cities of the Interior, pg. 249

· 2 ·

When she cooked, the entire kitchen was galvanized by the strength she put into it; the dishes, pans, knives, everything bore the brunt of her strength, everything was violently marshalled, challenged, forced to bloom, to cook, to boil. The vegetables were peeled as if the skins were torn from their resisting flesh, as they were the fur of animals being peeled by the hunters. The fruit was stabbed, assassinated, the lettuce murdered with a machete. The flavoring was poured like hot lava and one expected the salad to wither, shrivel instantly. The bread was sliced with a vigor which recalled heads falling from the guillotine. The bottles and glasses were knocked hard against each other as in bowling games, so that the wine, beer and water were conquered before they reached the table.

—Ladders to Fire, in Cities of the Interior, pg. 4

· 3 ·

Life is a process of becoming, a combination of states we have to go through. Where people fail is that they wish to elect a state and remain in it. This is a kind of death.

—*D. H. Lawrence: An Unprofessional Study*, pg. 20

· 4 ·

Ordinary life does not interest me. I seek only the high moments. I am in accord with the surrealists, searching for the marvelous.

—*Diary 1*, pg. 5

· 5 ·

You live like this, sheltered, in a delicate world,
and you believe you are living. Then you read a book
...or you take a trip...and you discover that you are
not living, that you are hibernating. The symptoms of
hibernating are easily detectable: first, restlessness.
The second symptom (when hibernating becomes
dangerous and might degenerate into death): absence
of pleasure. That is all. It appears like an innocuous illness.
Monotony, boredom, death. Millions live like this (or die
like this) without knowing it. They work in offices. They
drive a car. They picnic with their families. They raise
children. And then some shock treatment takes place, a
person, a book, a song, and it awakens them
and saves them from death. Some never awaken.

—*Diary 1*, pg. 7

· 6 ·

I always endowed madness with a sacred, poetic value, a mystical value. It seemed to me to be a denial of ordinary life, an effort to transcend it, to expand, to go far beyond the limitations of *La Condition Humaine*.

—Diary 1, pg. 40

· 7 ·

Idealism is the death of the body and the imagination.

—Diary 1, pg. 42

· 8 ·

All but freedom, utter freedom, is death.

—Diary 1, pg. 42

· 9 ·

I was upset as a child to discover that we only had one life. It seems to me that I wanted to compensate for this by multiplying experience.

—Diary 1, pg. 47

· 10 ·

Passion gives me moments of wholeness.

—Diary 1, pg. 48

· 11 ·

If what Proust says is true, that happiness is the absence of fever, then I will never know happiness. For I am possessed by a fever for knowledge, experience, and creation.

—Diary 1, pg. 65

· 12 ·

I have just stood before the open window of my bedroom and I have breathed in deeply all the honeysuckle-perfumed air, the sunshine, the snowdrops of winter, the crocuses of spring, the primroses, the crooning pigeons, the trills of the birds, the entire procession of soft winds and cool smells, of frail colors and petal-textured skies, the knotted snake greys of old vine roots, the vertical shoots of young branches, the dank smell of old leaves, of wet earth, of torn roots, and fresh-cut grass, winter, summer, and fall, sunrises and sunsets, storms and lulls, wheat and chestnuts, wild strawberries and wild roses, violets and damp logs, burnt fields and new poppies.

—Diary 1, pg. 68

· 13 ·

I don't really want to become normal, average, standard. I want merely to gain in strength, in the courage to live out my life more fully, enjoy more, experience more. I want to develop even more original and more unconventional traits.

—Diary 1, pg. 112

· 14 ·

I want to live only for ecstasy. Small doses, moderate loves, all half-shades, leave me cold. I like extravagance.

—*Diary 1*, pg. 174

· 15 ·

The same dress can be crumpled and worn to bed, the same brushed hair thrown to the winds, safety pins and hatpins can fall, heels of shoes can break. When a higher moment comes, all details recede into the background. I never lose sight of the whole. An impeccable dress is made to be lived in, to be torn, wet, stained, crumpled.

—*Diary 1*, pg. 184

· 16 ·

My surroundings are me. Everything is me, because I have rejected all conventions, the opinions of the world, all its laws.

—*Diary 1*, pp. 185-186

· 17 ·

I postpone death by living, by suffering, by error, by risking, by giving, by losing.

—*Diary 1*, pg. 190

· 18 ·

What interests me is not the core but the potentialities of this core to multiply and expand infinitely. The diffusion of the core, its suppleness and elasticity, rebound, ramifications. Spanning, encompassing, space-devouring, star-trodden journeys, everything around and between the core.

—Diary 1, pg. 201

· 19 ·

The personal life deeply lived always expands into truths beyond itself.

—Diary 2, pg. ix

· 20 ·

Paris, New York, the two magnetic poles of the world. Paris a sensual city which seduced the body, enlivened the senses, New York unnatural, synthetic; Paris-New York, the two high tension magnetic poles between life, life of the senses, of the spirit in Paris, and life in action in New York.

—Diary 2, pg. 7

· 21 ·

The discovery of significance is what deepens and embellishes experience.

—Diary 2, pg. 8

· 22 ·

I love the world so much, it moves me deeply, even the ordinary world, the daily world, even the bar table, the tinkling of ice in the glasses, the waiter, the dog tied in the coat room.

—Diary 2, pg. 34

· 23 ·

I cannot give superficially, can only form vital, deep attachments to a few. I hold back from the casual flow.

—Diary 2, pg. 38

· 24 ·

There is not one big cosmic meaning for all, there is only the meaning we each give to our life, an individual meaning, an individual plot, like an individual novel, a book for each person.

—Diary 2, pg. 45

· 25 ·

People living deeply have no fear of death.

—Diary 2, pg. 60

· 26 ·

I have decided to become reckless, to do and try everything because nothing holds me on earth, and I am not afraid to die.

—Diary 2, pg. 63

· 27 ·

I will live out my fantasies, intoxicate myself with people, life, noise, work, creation, even if it means a shorter life, for life is not worth dragging out too long.

—Diary 2, pg. 63

· 28 ·

In Spanish I hear things with my body, my senses, my blood, not with my mind. It reaches me through subterranean channels of atavistic memories. It touches a different Anaïs, one I scarcely know.

—Diary 2, pg. 86

· 29 ·

Dreams are necessary to life.

—Diary 2, pg. 89

· 30 ·

We often live moved by impulses which our wide-open eyes of consciousness know to be dangerous, perhaps fatal. We rush into ecstasies before lucidity overtakes us, and paralyzes us. Illusion gives us heightened joys unknown to pedestrians and realists. And these people who resist intoxication by the drugs of imagination or aesthetics are those who seek it out of wine bottles, or drugs like opium.

—Diary 2, pg. 127

· 31 ·

Life, for me, is a profound, a sacred, a joyous, a mysterious, a soulful dance. But it is a dance. Through the markets, the whorehouses, the abattoirs, the butcher shops, the scientific laboratories, hospitals, Montparnasse, I walk with my dream unfurled, and lose myself in my own labyrinths, and the dream unfurled carries me.

—Diary 2, pg. 152

· 32 ·

With a hammer and nails, paint, soap, money, typewriter, cookbook, douche bags, I created a dream.

—Diary 2, pg. 152

· 33 ·

How each friend represents a world in us, a world possibly not born until they arrive, and it is only by this meeting that a new world is born.

—Diary 2, pg. 193

· 34 ·

Fulfillment is the completion of a circle. All aspects of the self have to be lived out, like the twelve houses of the zodiac.

—Diary 2, pg. 249

· 35 ·

A personality is one who has unrolled the ribbon, unfolded the petals, exposed all the layers. It does not matter where one begins: with instinct or wisdom, with nature or spirit.

—Diary 2, pg. 249

· 36 ·

Fulfillment means the experience of all parts of the self, all the elements, all the planes. It means each cell of the body comes alive, awakened. One dies when the cells are exhausted, one reaches plenitude when they all function, the dream, desire, instinct, appetite. One awakens the other. It is like contagion. The order does not matter. All the errors are necessary, the stutterings, the blunders, the blindnesses. The end is to cover all the terrain, all the routes. No spaces to skip.

—Diary 2, pg. 249

· 37 ·

There is greatness only in fulfillment, in the fullness of awakening. Completion means the symphony.

—*Diary 2*, pg. 249

· 38 ·

Psychologically, a great personality is a circle touching something at every point. A circle with a core.

—*Diary 2*, pg. 249

· 39 ·

Life is a full circle, widening until it joins the circle motions of the infinite.

—*Diary 2*, pg. 249

· 40 ·

There are only two kinds of freedom in the world: the freedom of the rich and powerful, and the freedom of the artist and the monk who renounces possessions.

—*Diary 3*, pg. 22

· 41 ·

The earth is heavy and opaque without dreams.

—*Diary 3*, pg. 78

· 42 ·

A leaf fluttered in through the window this morning, as if supported by the rays of the sun, a bird settled on the fire escape, joy in the taste of the coffee, joy accompanied me as I walked...

—Diary 4, pg. 71

· 43 ·

Throw your dream into space like a kite, and you do not know what it will bring back, a new life, a new friend, a new love, a new country.

—Diary 4, pg. 74

· 44 ·

Dreams pass into the reality of action. From the actions stems the dream again; and this interdependence produces the highest form of living.

—Diary 4, pg. 150

· 45 ·

I know what my crime is: what human beings only dream, I acted out. I obeyed the dream.

—Diary 5, pg. 25

· 46 ·

What I cannot love, I overlook.

—Diary 5, pg. 120

· 47 ·

I seek to escape from the past. I prefer unfamiliar landscapes, unfamiliar atmospheres. I love change of setting, futuristic designs, changes of fashion, frequent metamorphosis, shedding of the past in all its forms.

—Diary 5, pg. 194

· 48 ·

After a while I discard a dress not because it is worn (I cannot wear out my dresses, I hardly fray them) but because of the self which enjoyed that particular dress has changed, has outworn it, needs to assume another color, another shape.

—Diary 5, pg. 194

· 49 ·

I would at times be less of a rebel if people did not seem so inert, cautious.

—Diary 5, pg. 214

· 50 ·

I will not be just a tourist in the world of images, just watching images passing by which I cannot live in, make love to, possess as permanent sources of joy and ecstasy.

—*Diary 5*, pg. 262

· 51 ·

My interpretation of the phrase "to take root" is negative; for me it means cutting off avenues of escape, of communication with the rest of the world. So that against the wish for repose, there is an impulse to remain mobile, fluid, to change surroundings.

—*Diary 6*, pg. 15

· 52 ·

You can fall in love with your father and brother. You can rebel against your mother. You can kill your rivals. You can steal others' loves. You can betray all your loves...in dreams. You can be amorous and orgiastic, you can be a thousand women, in your dreams. But enact one of them and you are a criminal in your own eyes, in the world's eyes, and you are condemned.

—*Diary 6*, pg. 25

· 53 ·

Most of my rebellions are against mediocrity.

—*Diary 6*, pg. 25

· 54 ·

Analysis is only to be used when needed. The rest of the time one should live passionately and impulsively, create and test one's strength.

—Diary 6, pg. 40

· 55 ·

Pleasure is an attitude, not a person or place.

—Diary 6, pg. 52

· 56 ·

We travel, some of us forever, to seek other states, other lives, other souls.

—Diary 7, pg. 98

· 57 ·

To withhold from living is to die...the more you give of yourself to life the more life nourishes you.

—Fire, pg. 212

· 58 ·

Ecstasy is the moment of exaltation from wholeness!

—Fire, pg. 293

· 59 ·

Abnormal pleasures kill the taste for normal ones.

—Eduardo Sanchez, quoted in *Henry & June*, pg. 4

· 60 ·

There is in me something untouched, unstirred, which commands me. That will have to be moved if I am to move wholly.

—*Henry & June*, pg. 8

· 61 ·

Everything with me is either worship and passion or pity and understanding. I hate rarely, though when I hate, I hate murderously. For example now, I hate the bank and everything connected with it. I also hate Dutch paintings, penis-sucking, parties, and cold rainy weather. But I am much more preoccupied with loving.

—*Henry & June*, pg. 13

· 62 ·

I do not need drugs, artificial stimulation. Yet I want to experience those very things with June, to penetrate the evil which attracts me.

—on June Miller, *Henry & June*, pg. 34

· 63 ·

Pain is something to master, not to wallow in.

—Henry & June, pg. 36

· 64 ·

Luxury is not a necessity to me, but beautiful and good things are.

—Henry & June, pg. 38

· 65 ·

The truth is that this is the only way I can live: in two directions. I need two lives. I am two beings.

—Henry & June, pg. 60

· 66 ·

What can I do with my happiness? How can I keep it, conceal it, bury it where I may never lose it? I want to kneel as it falls over me like rain, gather it up with lace and silk, and press it over myself again.

—Henry & June, pg. 167

· 67 ·

I want to bite into life, and to be torn by it.

—Henry & June, pg. 179

· 68 ·

The cabarets excite me. I want to hear raucous music, to see faces, to brush against bodies, to drink fiery Benedictine.

—*Henry & June*, pg. 179

· 69 ·

I want to dance. I want drugs. I want to know perverse people, to be intimate with them.

—*Henry & June*, pg. 179

· 70 ·

Am I hypnotized, fascinated by evil because I have none in me? Or is there in me the greatest secret evil?

—*Henry & June*, pg. 246

· 71 ·

And she danced; she danced with the music and with the rhythm of earth's circles; she turned with the earth turning, like a disk, turning all faces to the light and to darkness evenly, dancing towards daylight.

—*House of Incest*, pg. 72

· 72 ·

To commit suicide is easy. To live without a god is more difficult. The drunkenness of triumph is greater than the drunkenness of sacrifice.

—Incest, pg. 8

· 73 ·

I am overflowing. I talk too much. I love too much. I want to work. I like the confusion in my head because a whirlpool of feelings confuses my mind and destroys its control. I want to live by my feelings.

—Incest, pg. 242

· 74 ·

I seek the real stuff of life. Profound drama.

—Incest, pg. 305

· 75 ·

I am so thirsty for the marvelous that only the marvelous has power over me.

—Incest, pg. 350

· 76 ·

How flesh touching flesh generates a perfume, and the friction of words only pain and division. To formulate without destroying the mind, without tampering, without killing, without withering. That is what I have learned by living, that delicacy and awe of the senses. That respect for the perfume will become my law in art.

—*Incest*, pg. 361

· 77 ·

I cannot install myself definitely in human life. It is not enough. I must climb dizzier regions.

—*Incest*, pg. 403

· 78 ·

For a few moments of ecstasy I am always willing to endure the pain.

—*Mirages*, pg. 180

· 79 ·

My only reality is passion and its need of fulfillment.

—*Mirages*, pg. 182

· 80 ·

Passion pushes the sails and creates the currents of drama
and life and action.

—Mirages, pg. 195

· 81 ·

I regret no physical gesture ever made. My only regrets are
for those I did not make fully...

—Mirages, pg. 265

· 82 ·

I can immediately produce another love, another dream,
as fast as life dissolves them.

—Mirages, pg. 282

· 83 ·

Where do I get the psychic energy? What carries me where
others with my kind of body would collapse? The dream.

—Mirages, pg. 290

· 84 ·

Real wonder lies in the depths; as soon as you look deeply
you find the extraordinary.

—Mirages, pg. 335

· 85 ·

Do not be trapped by what you need—seek what you truly want.

—*Trapeze*, pg. 143

· 86 ·

I flipped my eyes, my billowy Italian dress and said: "My roots are portable."

—*Trapeze*, pg. 362

· 87 ·

I was always exhausted by my dreams, not because of the dreams, but because of the fear of not being able to return. I do not need to return. I will find you everywhere. You alone can go wherever I go, into the same mysterious regions. You too know the language of the nerves. You will always know what I am saying even if I do not.

—*Under a Glass Bell*, pg. 54

· 88 ·

The dream was always running ahead of one. To catch up, to live for a moment in unison with it, that was the miracle.

—*Winter of Artifice* (American edition), pg. 175

Lust for Life

LOVE AND SENSUALITY

· 89 ·

Love never dies a natural death. It dies because we don't
know how to replenish its source, it dies of blindness and
errors and betrayals. It dies of illness and wounds, it dies
of weariness, of witherings, of tarnishings, but never a
natural death.

— *The Four-Chambered Heart*, in *Cities of the Interior*, pg. 269

· 90 ·

No two caresses ever resemble each other. Every lover
holds a new body until he fills it with his essence, and no
two essences are the same, and no flavor is ever repeated.

— *The Four-Chambered Heart*, in *Cities of the Interior*, pg. 281

· 91 ·

The enemy of a love is never outside, it's not a man or
woman, it's what we lack in ourselves.

— *A Spy in the House of Love*, in *Cities of the Interior*, pg. 459

· 92 ·

Only the united beat of sex and heart together can
create ecstasy.

— *Delta of Venus*, pg. xiv

· 93 ·

He was now in that state of fire that she loved. She wanted to be burnt.

—Delta of Venus, pg. 152

· 94 ·

If I love you it means we share the same fantasies, the same madnesses.

—Diary 1, pg. 22

· 95 ·

The love of only one man or one woman is a limitation.

—Diary 1, pg. 42

· 96 ·

The truly faithless one is the one who makes love to only a fraction of you. And denies the rest.

—Diary 1, pg. 51

· 97 ·

The body is an instrument which only gives off music when it is used as a body. Always an orchestra, and just as music traverses walls, so sensuality traverses the body and reaches up to ecstasy.

—Diary 2, pg. 36

Love and Sensuality

· 98 ·

Someday I'll be locked up for love insanity. "She loved too much."

—*Diary 2*, pg. 205

· 99 ·

I will never be able to describe the states of dazzlement, the trances, the ecstasies produced in my by love-making. More than communion, more than any joy in writing, more than the infinite, life in the unity achieved by passion. It is the only moment when I am at rest, that is the summit, the miracle.

—*Diary 2*, pg. 251

· 100 ·

Electric flesh-arrows traversing the body. A rainbow of color strikes the eyelids. A foam of music falls over the ears. It is the gong of the orgasm.

—*Diary 2*, pg. 264

· 101 ·

You cannot save people, you can only love them. You cannot transform them, you can only console them.

—*Diary 2*, pg. 338

· 102 ·

Anxiety is love's greatest killer. It creates the failures. It makes others feel as you might when a drowning man holds on to you. You want to save him, but you know he will strangle you with his panic.

—Diary 4, pg. 185

· 103 ·

You shouldn't flirt with a woman who doesn't know how to flirt.

—said to Henry Miller in *Henry & June*, pg. 7

· 104 ·

There are two ways to reach me: by way of kisses or by way of the imagination. But there is a hierarchy: the kisses alone don't work.

—Henry & June, pg. 8

· 105 ·

For you and for me the highest moment, the keenest joy, is not when our minds dominate but when we lose our minds, and you and I both lose it in the same way, through love.

—Henry & June, pg. 47

· 106 ·

Your voice reverberates against my body like another kind of caress, another kind of penetration.

—Henry & June, pg. 66

· 107 ·

Do not seek the because—in love there is no because, no reason, no explanation, no solutions.

—Henry & June, pg. 90

· 108 ·

He guides my inexperienced hands. It is like a forest fire, to be with him. New places of my body are aroused and burnt. He is incendiary. I leave him in an unquenchable fever.

—Henry & June, pg. 101

· 109 ·

I have never been able to conceal from a man that I loved him.

—Henry & June, pg. 174

· 110 ·

Love reduces the complexity of living.

—Henry & June, pg. 178

· 111 ·

I have only three desires now, to eat, to sleep, and to fuck.

—Henry & June, pg. 179

· 112 ·

It is easy to love and there are so many ways to do it.

—Henry & June, pg. 211

· 113 ·

I hated him because I loved him as I had never loved anyone.

—Henry & June, pg. 217

· 114 ·

Men look at me and I look at them, with my being unlocked. No more veils.

—Henry & June, pg. 221

· 115 ·

I cannot live without love. Love is at the root of my being.

—Henry & June, pg. 266

Love and Sensuality

· 116 ·

I want to live only for the love of man, and as an artist
—as a mistress, as a creator.

—Incest, pg. 330

· 117 ·

Oh, God, I know no joy as great as the moment of rushing
into a new love, no ecstasy like that of a new love. I swim
in the sky; I float; my body is full of flowers, flowers
with fingers giving me acute, acute caresses, sparks,
jewels, quivers of joy, dizziness, such dizziness. Music
inside of one, drunkenness. Only closing the eyes and
remembering, and the hunger, the hunger for more, more,
the great hunger, the voracious hunger, and thirst.

—Incest, pp. 334-335

· 118 ·

Love is the axis and breath of my life. The art I produce is
a byproduct, an excrescence of love, the song I sing, the
joy which must explode, the overabundance—that is all!

—Incest, pg. 395

· 119 ·

I am the celestial Madame, and this world will castrate me
unless I find a MAN for myself soon.

—Mirages, pg. 250

· 120 ·

One loves in proportion to one's vision. I see more, so
I love more.

—*Mirages*, pg. 293

· 121 ·

He was ardent, sensual, potent. I forgot his ugliness.

—on Edmund Wilson, *Mirages*, pg. 295

· 122 ·

My body receives his movements. I feel suddenly melted
in his mouth, or I feel the neatness of his hips, his legs
against or within my own. If only he felt this.

—on Gore Vidal, *Mirages*, pg. 328

· 123 ·

Gore took me to dinner. In the middle of the dinner he
said: "I wonder if there could be a marriage without sex."

—on Gore Vidal, *Mirages*, pg. 332

· 124 ·

Gore, my love, I lie here listening to music and so filled
with you that I marvel that an incomplete love should
seem so complete.

—on Gore Vidal, *Mirages*, pg. 337

Love and Sensuality

· 125 ·

By erotic I mean the totality of sexual experience, its atmosphere, mood, sensual flavors, mystery, vibrations, the state of ecstasy into which it may plunge us, the full range of the senses and emotions which accompany, surround it, and which the explicit flat clinical descriptions destroy.

—*The Novel of the Future*, pg. 178

· 126 ·

I leap at his arrival. The current is so strong, current of fire and of water, of nerves, and of mists, of mysteries.

—on Rupert Pole, *Trapeze*, pg. 37

· 127 ·

How the lies and the loves, and the dreams, and the obscenities and the fevers weighed down her body, and how I wanted to become leadened with her, poisoned with her!

—*The Winter of Artifice* (1939 edition), pp. 103-104

· 128 ·

Pounding of drums. Delirious sensual diffusions. Effulgence of face and breasts.

—*The Winter of Artifice* (1939 edition), pg. 104

CONSCIOUSNESS

· 129 ·

The dreamer rejects the ordinary.

—*Children of the Albatross*, in *Cities of the Interior*, pg. 219

· 130 ·

If you take all your fears, one by one, make a list of them, face them, decide to challenge them, most of them will vanish.

—*Seduction of the Minotaur*, in *Cities of the Interior*, pg. 491

· 131 ·

We do not see things as they are, we see them as we are.

—*Seduction of the Minotaur*, in *Cities of the Interior*, pg. 578

· 132 ·

Human beings can reach such desperate solitude that they may cross a boundary beyond which words cannot serve, and at such moments there is nothing left for them but to *bark*.

—*Collages*, pg. 116

· 133 ·

Human beings place upon an object, or a person, this responsibility of being the obstacle when the obstacle lies always within one's self.

—*Diary 1*, pg. 4

· 134 ·

My life is slowed up by thought and the need to understand what I am living.

—*Diary 1*, pg. 48

· 135 ·

I have such a great need of truth! It must be that need of immediate recording which incites me to write almost while I am living, before it is altered, changed by distance or time.

—*Diary 1*, pg. 65

· 136 ·

Enter this laboratory of the soul where incidents are refracted into a diary, dissected to prove that every one of us carries a deforming mirror where he sees himself too small or too large, too fat or too thin… Once the deforming mirror is smashed, there is a possibility of wholeness; there is a possibility of joy.

—*Diary 1*, pg. 105

· 137 ·

In my childhood diary I wrote: "I have decided that it is better not to love anyone, because when you love people, then you have to be separated from them, and that hurts too much."

—*Diary 1*, pg. 115

· 138 ·

The basis of insincerity is the idealized image we hold of ourselves and wish to impose on others—an admirable image.

—*Diary 1*, pg. 128

· 139 ·

The possession of knowledge does not kill the sense of wonder and mystery. There is always more mystery.

—*Diary 1*, pg. 155

· 140 ·

Lies create solitude.

—*Diary 1*, pg. 163

· 141 ·

There were always in me, two women at least, one woman
desperate and bewildered, who felt she was drowning,
and another who only wanted to bring beauty, grace, and
aliveness to people and who would leap into a scene, as
upon a stage, conceal her true emotions because they were
weaknesses, helplessness, despair, and present to the world
only a smile, an eagerness, curiosity, enthusiasm, interest.

—Diary 1, pg. 270

· 142 ·

When others asked the truth of me, I was convinced it was
not the truth they wanted, but an illusion they could bear
to live with.

—Diary 1, pg. 286

· 143 ·

For me, the adventures of the mind, each inflection of
thought, each movement, nuance, growth, discovery, is a
source of exhilaration.

—Diary 1, pg. 295

· 144 ·

Perhaps I stopped loving my father long ago. What
remained was slavery to a pattern.

—Diary 1, pg. 318

Consciousness

· 145 ·

We love best those who are, or act for us, a self we do not wish to be or act out.

—*Diary 1*, pg. 330

· 146 ·

The life of the unconscious is the life without pattern, continuity, or rigidity. It approximates the dream. It is pure flow.

—*Diary 1*, pg. 331

· 147 ·

I was thinking of my patients, and how the worst moment for them was when they discovered they were masters of their own fate. It was not a matter of bad or good luck. When they could no longer blame fate, they were in despair.

—on psychoanalysis, *Diary 2*, pp. 30-31

· 148 ·

In the interior monologue there is no punctuation.

—*Diary 2*, pg. 53

· 149 ·

Neurosis causes a perpetual double exposure. It can only be erased by daylight, by an isolated confrontation of it, as if it were a ghost which demanded visibility and once having been pulled out into the daylight it dies.

—*Diary 2*, pg. 58

· 150 ·

Introspection is a devouring monster. You have to feed it with much material, much experience, many people, many places, many loves, many creations, and then it ceases feeding on you.

—Diary 2, pg. 81

· 151 ·

Chaos, storms, furies, anguish, they come as fiercely as in all women but very quickly I swim to the surface, and I can see with human eyes, and control the damage of primitive floods and eruptions.

—Diary 2, pg. 230

· 152 ·

When you live closely to individual dramas you marvel that we do not have continuous war, knowing what nightmares human beings conceal, what secret obsessions and hidden cruelties.

—Diary 2, pg. 346

· 153 ·

Life shrinks or expands in proportion to one's courage.

—Diary 3, pg. 125

· 154 ·

You are crossing a street. The automobile does not strike you down. It is not you who are inside the ambulance being taken to St. Vincent's Hospital. It is not you whose mother died. Not you whose brother went to war and was killed. In all the registers of catastrophe your name does not appear. You were not attacked, raped, mutilated. You were not on the clipper which sank into the sea with twenty passengers. You were not in a concentration camp, not on the refugee ship which was not permitted to land anywhere... None of that.

But as you cross the street the wind lifts the dirt and before it touches your face you feel as if all these horrors have happened to you, you feel the nameless anxiety, the shrinking of the heart, the asphyxiation, the suffocation of pain, the horror of the soul being stabbed. Invisible drama. Every other illness is understood, shared with other human beings. Not this one. It is mysterious and solitary, it is ineffectual and unmoving to others as the attempted crying out of a mute person.

Everybody understands hunger, physical pain, illness, poverty, slavery. But no one understands that this moment at which I crossed the street is more annihilating than a concrete catastrophe. Anxiety is a woman screaming without a voice, out of a nightmare.

—Diary 3, pg. 276

· 155 ·

There are very few human beings who receive the truth, complete and staggering, by instant illumination. Most of them acquire it fragment by fragment, on a small scale, by successive developments, cellularly, like a laborious mosaic.

—Diary 3, pg. 294

· 156 ·

When anxiety sets in like a fever, cold and hot waves, chills, be calm. Know it for what it is: anxiety. Do not explain it away by blaming any particular incident, experience, for then it becomes magnified. When depression suffocates you like a London fog, think that the cause is not as great as you may think. A small defeat, a small frustration, a small discord may set it off. You must see the transitoriness of moods. Beware of exaggerated reactions to harshness, brutality, ignorance, selfishness. Beware of allowing a tactless word, a rebuttal, a rejection to obliterate the whole sky.

—Diary 3, page 307

· 157 ·

When we blindly adopt a religion, a political system, a literary dogma, we become automatons. We cease to grow.

—Diary 4, pg. 10

· 158 ·

We do not grow absolutely, chronologically. We grow sometimes in one dimension, and not in another, unevenly. We grow partially. We are relative. We are mature in one realm, childish in another. The past, present, and future mingle and pull us backward, forward, or fix us in the present. We are made of layers, cells, constellations.

—Diary 4, pg. 127

· 159 ·

We never discard our childhood. We never escape it completely. We relive fragments of it through others. We live buried layers through others. We live through others' projections of the unlived selves.

—Diary 4, pg. 127

· 160 ·

The corpse of our human love is illumined and kept alive by our first illusion, and one is uneasy at burying it, doubting its death. Will it rise again and remain a part of our life forever?

—Diary 5, pg. 33

· 161 ·

It is not imagination which stirs in the blood obscurely at certain spectacles, certain cities, certain faces; it is memory.

—Diary 5, pg. 37

· 162 ·

We do not remain smaller in stature than our parents. Nature had intended them to shrink progressively while we reach for our own maturity.

—Diary 5, pg. 40

· 163 ·

Occasionally, I think of death. I can easily believe in the disintegration of the body, but cannot believe that all I have learned, experienced, accumulated, can disappear and be wasted. Like a river, it must flow somewhere.

—Diary 5, pg. 48

· 164 ·

The suppression of inner patterns in favor of patterns created by society is dangerous to us.

—Diary 5, pg. 56

· 165 ·

When we totally accept a pattern not made by us, not truly our own, we wither and die.

—Diary 5, pg. 57

· 166 ·

What we cannot see within ourselves, what we cannot seize within ourselves we project outside. A great part of our life is an invention to avoid confrontation with our deepest self.

—Diary 5, pg. 83

· 167 ·

With analysis there is the pain of breaking through, of pushing out. It is a rebirth. Only it has to be done by one's self, not the mother.

—Diary 5, pg. 147

· 168 ·

When you make a world tolerable for yourself, you make a world tolerable for others.

—Diary 5, pg. 149

· 169 ·

What a burden of guilt when a mother serves you, does all the menial tasks, feeds you, works for you, but then does not approve of what we become.

—Diary 5, pg. 177

· 170 ·

Maturity is first shedding of what you are not, and then the balancing of what you are in relation to the human being you love, and allowing the selves of that person which are not related to you to exist independently.

—Diary 5, pg. 196

· 171 ·

When you give someone a flavor of other worlds, you also give the poison of discontent.

—Diary 5, pg. 229

· 172 ·

The habits you cannot bear in others are those you fight against in yourself.

—Diary 5, pg. 230

· 173 ·

What we project onto others and they onto us is bound to be destructive because it is a fantasy.

—Diary 5, pg. 232

· 174 ·

We are like sculptors, constantly carving out of others the image we long for, need, love or desire. Often against reality, against their benefit, and always, in the end, a disappointment because it does not fit them.

—Diary 6, pp. 17-18

· 175 ·

I always like to write by the cold, clear light of airplane cloudscapes... It is intensely white, sharp. But if I see everything clearly in this light it is not because of the light itself but the altitude and separation from those I love.

—Diary 6, pg. 27

· 176 ·

People think this exploration of self is self-centered and selfish, but I notice that whenever I clear up something for myself it quickly affects everyone around me, as if it were a psychic liberation which in turn affects others' conflicts... It is more powerful than the self-sacrifice of the so-called selfless ones.

—Diary 6, pg. 61

· 177 ·

By cutting off friendships you create your own solitude.

—Diary 6, pg. 203

· 178 ·

I have the power to multiply myself. I am not one woman.

—Early Diary 4, pg. 193

· 179 ·

Experience teaches acceptance of the imperfect as life.

—Fire, pp. 202-203

· 180 ·

I have an attitude now that is immovable. I shall remain outside of the world, beyond the temporal, beyond all the organizations of the world. I only believe in poetry.

—Fire, pg. 285

· 181 ·

I will always be the virgin-prostitute, the perverse angel, the two-faced sinister and saintly woman.

—Henry & June, pg. 2

· 182 ·

Nothing too long imagined can be perfect in a worldly way.

—Henry & June, pg. 24

· 183 ·

Sometimes we reveal ourselves when we are least like ourselves.

—Henry & June, pg. 24

· 184 ·

I see myself wrapped in lies, which do not seem to penetrate my soul, as if they are not really a part of me. They are like costumes.

—Henry & June, pg. 231

· 185 ·

To lie, of course, is to engender insanity.

—Henry & June, pg. 231

· 186 ·

One does not learn to suffer less but to dodge pain.

—Henry & June, pg. 234

· 187 ·

Last night I wept. I wept because the process by which I have become woman was painful. I wept because I was no longer a child with a child's blind faith. I wept because my eyes were opened to reality... I wept because I could not believe anymore and I love to believe. I can still love passionately without believing. That means I love humanly. I wept because from now on I will weep less. I wept because I have lost my pain and I am not yet accustomed to its absence.

—Henry & June, pg. 274

· 188 ·

Worlds self made are so full of monsters and demons.

—*House of Incest*, pg. 30

· 189 ·

The trouble with anger is that it makes us overstate our case and prevents us from reaching awareness.

—*In Favor of the Sensitive Man*, pg. 30

· 190 ·

Group thinking does not give us strength. It weakens the will. Majority thinking is oppressive because it inhibits individual growth and seeks a formula for all.

—*In Favor of the Sensitive Man*, pg. 32

· 191 ·

I am like a snake who has already bitten. I retreat from a direct battle while knowing the slow effect of the poison.

—*Incest*, pg. 20

Consciousness

· 192 ·

I disregard the proportions, the measures, the tempo of the ordinary world. I refuse to live in the ordinary world as an ordinary woman. To enter ordinary relationships. I want ecstasy. I am a neurotic—in the sense that I live in my world. I will not adjust myself to the world. I am adjusted to myself.

—*Incest*, pg. 134

· 193 ·

I only believe in intoxication, in ecstasy, and when ordinary life shackles me, I escape, one way or another. No more walls.

—*Incest*, pg. 350

· 194 ·

The dream is my only life. I seek in the echoes and reverberations the transfiguration which alone keeps wonder pure. Otherwise all magic is lost.

—*Incest*, pg. 366

· 195 ·

Fear alone causes jealousy.

—*Mirages*, pg. 51

· 196 ·

The secret of joy is the mastery of pain.

—*Mirages*, pg. 287

· 197 ·

Strength is a rhythm, not an absolute.

—*Mirages*, pg. 332

· 198 ·

The human being we relate to best is the one who reflects our present psychic state.

—*Mirages*, pg. 352

· 199 ·

Aging is not a physical phenomenon. It comes when one wearies of repetitious motifs.

—*Mirages*, pg. 393

· 200 ·

Neurosis was caused by our attempt to separate physical and metaphysical levels, to set them up in opposition to each other, thus engaging in an internecine war.

—*The Novel of the Future*, pg. 6

· 201 ·

Passivity...is destructive to human life and to art.

—The Novel of the Future, pg. 11

· 202 ·

Our psychological reality, which lies below the surface, frightens us because it endlessly surprises us and drives us in a direction which society's rules and organizations define as wrong or dangerous. When experiencing such fears, the conscious mind tries first of all the control the unconscious by repression. When it cannot be repressed, it rebels. When it rebels, it may lead either to madness or to life.

—The Novel of the Future, pg. 43

· 203 ·

It takes courage to face the mobility and fluidity of life. It means confronting the undiscovered areas and the ones we have stored in the attic for the sake of tidiness.

—The Novel of the Future, pg. 65

· 204 ·

Alienation from the self means alienation from others.

—The Novel of the Future, pg. 73

· 205 ·

Each person possesses a rich interior world which we are unable to share because we do not take the trouble to explore it.

—*The Novel of the Future*, pg. 132

· 206 ·

The outside (nature) cannot give us what we do not possess within.

—*The Novel of the Future*, pg. 141

· 207 ·

Men who live only by habit and routine die.

—*The Novel of the Future*, pg. 170

· 208 ·

Depth alone is what gives perspective to the universal. It is not numerical growth or gigantic physical dimensions which give stature to man.

—*The Novel of the Future*, pg. 195

· 209 ·

We are born with the power to alter what we are given at birth.

—The Novel of the Future, pg. 197

· 210 ·

The criminal destroys the innocent instead of destroying the world he hates in himself.

—The Novel of the Future, pg. 197

· 211 ·

We are always forcing others to be what we want, need, imagine, and we never forgive them for being themselves.

—Trapeze, pg. 138

· 212 ·

Nothing more tragic in the world than the walls of China that grow between human beings, and the real priest is the one who dissolves them.

—Trapeze, pg. 173

· 213 ·

We live in fragments. The design is only revealed later.

—Trapeze, pg. 189

· 214 ·

Guilt is self-censorship—to become free of it means to accept one's self as one is, and reality of one's acts.

—*Trapeze*, pg. 203

· 215 ·

Guilt produces anger at the one who causes it—a self-defensive anger.

—*Trapeze*, pg. 221

· 216 ·

We know that in ourselves the romantic, the bohemian, the adventurer never truly dies: it is suppressed.

—*Trapeze*, pg. 353

· 217 ·

Stupidity is not an excuse for hostility.

—*Trapeze*, pg. 360

· 218 ·

Rebellion is a negative expression of independence.

—*Trapeze*, pg. 378

· 219 ·

All those who try to unveil the mysteries always have tragic lives. At the end they are always punished.

—*Under a Glass Bell*, pg. 44

· 220 ·

Blame is never to be placed on one person. Every relationship is dialectical. Every relationship is interactive.

—unpublished diary, 1941

· 221 ·

No mistress can open a man's eyes to the pretenses of a wife!

—unpublished diary, 1941

· 222 ·

It is the romantic who cannot accept the failure of the absolute, who clings to dead loves and mutilated relationships.

—unpublished diary, 1943

· 223 ·

Character is as much revealed by what we fear as by what we manifest.

—unpublished diary, 1955

· 224 ·

It is astonishing how hostilities cease as you clarify
your projections.

—unpublished diary, 1955

· 225 ·

When one is pretending the entire body revolts.

—The Winter of Artifice (1939 edition), pg. 194

WOMEN AND MEN

· 226 ·

Nothing more difficult to live up to than men's dreams.

—*Children of the Albatross*, in *Cities of the Interior*, pg. 201

· 227 ·

I had a feeling that Pandora's box contained the mysteries of woman's sensuality, so different from a man's and for which man's language was inadequate. The language of sex had yet to be invented. The language of the senses was yet to be explored.

—*Delta of Venus*, pg. xi

· 228 ·

The love between women is a refuge and an escape into harmony and narcissism in place of conflict. In the love between man and woman there is resistance and conflict. Two women do not judge each other. They form an alliance. It is in a way, self-love.

—*Diary 1*, pg. 41

· 229 ·

Man can never know the kind of loneliness a woman knows. Man lies in a woman's womb only to gather strength, he nourishes himself from this fusion, and then he rises and goes into the world, into his work, into battle, into art. He is not lonely. He is busy. The memory of the swim in amniotic fluid gives him energy, completion. The woman may be busy too, but she feels empty. Sensuality for her is not only a wave of pleasure in which she has bathed, and a charge of electric joy at contact with another. When man lies in her womb, she is fulfilled, each act of love is a taking of man within her, an act of birth and rebirth, of child-bearing and man-bearing. Man lies in her womb and is reborn each time anew with a desire to act, to BE. But for a woman, the climax is not in the birth, but in the moment when man rests inside of her.

—Diary 1, pg. 106

· 230 ·

It's right for a woman to be, above all, human. I am a woman first of all.

—Diary 1, pg. 223

· 231 ·

What I have to say is really distinct from the artist and art: *it is the woman who has to speak*. And it is not only the woman Anaïs who has to speak, but I who have to speak for many women.

—Diary 1, pg. 289

· 232 ·

I see whole cycle of creation closing upon woman, the study of woman. I see all the roads of philosophy, the history of art, morphology, psychology, all converging to clear up the mystery of woman.

—Diary 1, pg. 333

· 233 ·

Psychoanalysis did save me because it allowed the birth of the real me, a most dangerous one for a woman, filled with dangers; for no one has loved an adventurous woman as they have loved adventurous men.

—Diary 1, pg. 361

· 234 ·

Men think they live and die for ideas. What a divine joke. They live and die for emotional, personal errors, just as women do.

—Diary 2, pg. 145

· 235 ·

If today I can talk both woman's and man's language, if I can translate woman to man and man to woman, it is because I do not believe in man's objectivity...all his ideas, systems, philosophies, arts come from a personal source he does not wish to admit.

—Diary 2, pg. 233

· 236 ·

Woman does not forget she needs the fecundator, she does not forget that everything that is born of her is planted in her.

—Diary 2, pg. 234

· 237 ·

Woman is not deluded. She must create without these proud delusions of man, without megalomania, without schizophrenia, without madness. She must create that unity which man first destroyed by his proud consciousness.

—Diary 2, pg. 234

· 238 ·

Woman was born to *be* the connecting link between man and his human self. Between abstract ideas and the personal pattern which creates them. Man, to create, must become man.

—Diary 2, pg. 234

· 239 ·

Woman's role in creation should be parallel to her role in life. I don't mean the good earth. I mean the bad earth too, the demon, the instincts, the storms of nature. Tragedies, conflicts, mysteries are personal. Man fabricated a detachment which became fatal. Woman must not fabricate. She must descend into the real womb and expose its secrets and its labyrinths. She must describe it as the city of Fez, with its Arabian Nights gentleness, tranquility and mystery. She must describe the voracious moods, the desires, the worlds contained in each cell of it. For the womb has dreams. It is not as simple as the good earth. I believe at times that man created art out of fear of exploring woman. I believe woman stuttered about herself out of fear of what she had to say. She covered herself with taboos and veils. Man invented a woman to suit his needs. He disposed of her by identifying her with nature and then paraded his contemptuous domination of nature. But woman is not nature only. She is the mermaid with her fish-tail dipped in the unconscious.

—Diary 2, pg. 235

· 240 ·

It is the source of woman's rebellions, her helplessness and dependency.

—Diary 5, pg. 70

· 241 ·

If my lover is irritating I will think what a beautiful alibi he gives me for going on a journey.

—Diary 6, pg. 11

· 242 ·

If my lover talks too much I will look out of the window and listen to the rain and think how well they synchronize.

—*Diary 6*, pg. 11

· 243 ·

Everything but happiness is neurosis. So speaks the man of wisdom, not the man of experience.

—*Fire*, pg. 203

· 244 ·

I have to live my life by mysterious laws, but I want to give to each man the illusion he needs, of loyalty, of exclusivity.

—*Fire*, pg. 393

· 245 ·

I hate men who are afraid of women's strength.

—*Henry & June*, pg. 18

· 246 ·

To retreat is not feminine, male, or trickery. It is a terror before utter destruction.

—*Henry & June*, pg. 65

· 247 ·

The passivity of the woman's role weighs on me, suffocates me. Rather than wait for his pleasure, I would like to take it, to run wild. Is it that which pushes me into lesbianism? It terrifies me.

—Henry & June, pg. 101

· 248 ·

It isn't strong women who make men weak, but weak men who make women overstrong.

—Henry & June, pg. 183

· 249 ·

What a man wants (what a man wants!) is to believe that a woman can love him so much that no other man can interest her.

—Henry & June, pg. 230

· 250 ·

I, with a deeper instinct, choose a man who compels my strength, who makes enormous demands, who has the courage to treat me like a woman.

—Henry & June, pg. 267

· 251 ·

Men complain that women demand reassurance or expressions of love. The Japanese recognized this, and in ancient times it was an absolute rule that after a night of lovemaking, the man had to produce a poem and have it delivered to his love before she awakened. What was this but the linking of lovemaking to love?

—*In Favor of the Sensitive Man*, pg. 3

· 252 ·

No one but a woman in love ever sees the maximum of men's greatness.

—*Incest*, pg. 344

· 253 ·

Motherhood is a vocation like any other. It should be freely chosen, not imposed upon woman.

—*Mirages*, pg. 26

· 254 ·

Man has been woman's only image of strength, her only ideal of strength. It is time for *her creation*.

—*Mirages*, pg. 199

· 255 ·

The man who has made the definitive conquest of nature, the American man, is the one most afraid of woman as nature, of the feminine in himself.

—The Novel of the Future, pg. 39

· 256 ·

The man who proceeds like a woman, in leaps, is the artist, the creative scientist, and the inventor. It was also a man who invented psychology, the science of dealing with the irrational.

—The Novel of the Future, pg. 39

· 257 ·

An armed man does not arouse human love.

—Trapeze, pg. 216

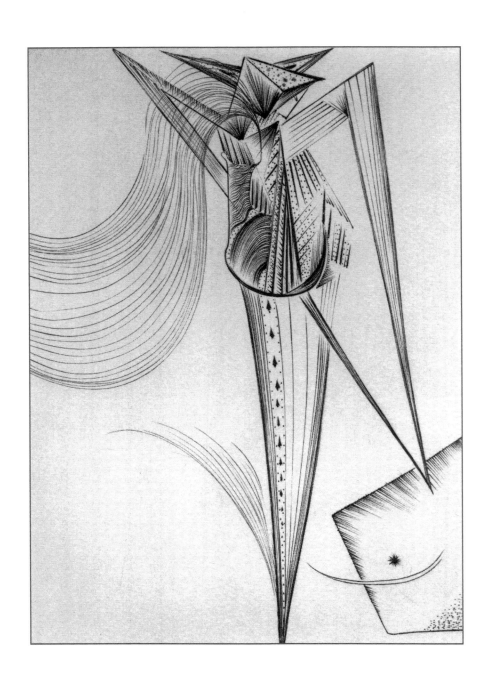

WRITING AND ART

· 258 ·

Finding one's self in a book is a second birth.

—*Collages*, pg. 114

· 259 ·

I am aware of being in a beautiful prison, from which I can only escape by writing.

—*Diary 1*, pg. 7

· 260 ·

I have always believed in André Breton's freedom, to write as one thinks, in the order and disorder in which one feels and thinks, to follow sensations and absurd correlations of events and images, to trust the new realms they lead one into.

—*Diary 1*, pg. 11

· 261 ·

We don't have a language for the senses. Feelings are images, sensations are like musical sounds.

—*Diary 1*, pg. 51

· 262 ·

To me the truth is something which cannot be told in
a few words, and those who simplify the universe only
reduce the expansion of its meaning.

—Diary 1, pg. 73

· 263 ·

Writers do not live one life, they live two. There is the
living and then there is the writing. There is the second
tasting, the delayed reaction.

—Diary 1, pg. 73

· 264 ·

How to defeat this tragedy concealed within each
hour, which chokes us unexpectedly and treacherously,
springing at us from a melody, an old letter, the colors of a
dress, the walk of a stranger? Make literature.

—Diary 1, pg. 128

· 265 ·

When life becomes too difficult, I turn to my work. I swim
into a new region.

—Diary 1, pg. 128

· 266 ·

Create a world, your world. Alone. Stand alone. Create.
And then the love will come to you, then it comes to you.
It was only when I wrote my first book that the world I
wanted to live in opened to me.

—Diary 1, pg. 185

· 267 ·

The diary began as a diary of a journey, to record
everything for my father. It was written for him, and I
had intended to send it to him. It was really a letter, so he
could follow us into a strange land, know about us. It was
also to be an island, in which I could take refuge in an
alien land, write French, think my thoughts, hold on to my
soul, to myself.

—Diary 1, 202

· 268 ·

This diary proves a tremendous, all engulfing craving for
truth since, to write it, I risk destroying the whole edifice
of my illusions, all the gifts I made, all that I created and
protected, everyone I saved from truth.

—Diary 1, pg. 242

· 269 ·

What does the world need, the illusion I give in life, or the truth I give in writing? When I went about dreaming of satisfying people's dreams, satisfying their hunger for illusion, didn't I know that this was the most painful and most insatiable hunger?

—Diary 1, pg. 242

· 270 ·

Perhaps I have loved the artist because creation is the nearest we come to divinity.

—Diary 1, pg. 261

· 271 ·

Here lies the personal overflow, the personal and feminine overfulness. Feelings that are not for books, not for fiction, not for art. All that I want to enjoy, not transform. My life has been one long series of efforts, self-discipline, will. Here I can sketch, improvise, be free, and myself.

—Diary 1, pg. 289

· 272 ·

The fear that truth should prove uninteresting is known only to weak-stomached artists. Respect the mysteries, they say. Do not open Pandora's box. Poetic vision is not the outcome of blindness but of a force which can transcend the ugliest face of reality, swallow and dissolve it by its strength, not evasion.

—Diary 1, pg. 292

· 273 ·

This diary is my kief, hashish and opium pipe. This is my drug and my vice.

—Diary 1, pg. 333

· 274 ·

Oh, the joy, the joy of writing, a joy so intense, so pure, so all-absorbing and free and all-encompassing, flooding the soul in mystical ecstasy, elevating and sanctifying, infusing beauty in the humblest subjects and a purpose in the most wayward life.

—Diary 2, pg. 8

· 275 ·

The poet is in love, a lover. The philosopher is a commentator.

—Diary 2, pg. 16

· 276 ·

The surrealists are the only ones who believed we could live by superimpositions, express it, layer upon layer, past and present, dream and actuality, because they believe we are not one dimensional, we do not exist or experience on one level alone, and that the only way to transcend the contradictions of life is to allow them to exist in such a multilateral state.

—Diary 2, pg. 58

· 277 ·

The artist really seeks a universal language, and artists from all parts of the world can understand each other.

—*Diary 2*, pg. 101

· 278 ·

I am like the crystal in which people find their mystic unity. Because of my obsession with essentials, my disregard of details, trivialities, interferences, contingencies, appearances, façades, disguises, gazing into me is like crystal-gazing. They see their fate, their potential self, secrets, their secret self.

—*Diary 2*, pg. 109

· 279 ·

The drug of poetry is far more potent than bare analysis. The drug of poetry makes truth and lucidity more absorbent. The intellect cannot resist its invasion. Language becomes the magic potion. Rhythm because the instrument of contagion, and the fluidity of the images flows directly into the subconscious without interference.

—*Diary 2*, pg. 127

· 280 ·

The monster I have to kill every day is realism. The monster who attacks me every day is destruction. Out of these duels comes transformation. I have to turn destruction into creation over and over again.

—*Diary 2*, pg. 145

Writing and Art

· 281 ·

Examine the past of most people and you find a neat cemetery or an urn with ashes. But examine the past of an artist and you find monuments to its perpetuity, a book, a statue, a painting, a symphony, a poem.

—Diary 2, pg. 169

· 282 ·

Poverty is the great reality. That is why the artist seeks it.

—Diary 2, pg. 201

· 283 ·

I am not interested in fiction. I want faithfulness.

—Diary 2, pg. 233

· 284 ·

All my creation is an effort to weave a web of connection with the world; I am always weaving it because it was once broken.

—Diary 3, pg. 231

· 285 ·

I write emotional algebra.

—Diary 4, pg. 151

· 286 ·

To write is to descend, to excavate, to go underground.

—Diary 5, pg. 41

· 287 ·

A trite word is an overused word which has lost its identity like an old coat in a second-hand shop. The familiar grows dull and we no longer see, hear, or taste it.

—Diary 5, pg. 56

· 288 ·

The artist sacrifices a great deal of security, peace of mind, for the perpetual adventure, for the discovery of new colors, new words, new horizons, new territories of experience.

—Diary 5, pg. 56

· 289 ·

We must protect minority writers because they are the research workers of literature. They keep it alive.

—Diary 5, pg. 56

Writing and Art

· 290 ·

Artistic revolt, innovation, experiment should not be met with hostility. They may disturb an established order or an artificial conventionality, but they may rescue us from death in life, from robot life, from boredom, from loss of the self, from enslavement.

—Diary 5, pp. 56-57

· 291 ·

I realized the vital necessity of art. Human life, yes, you nurse people, you clean house, you market, but then comes the moment of solace and flight. I sit and write and summon other friends, other forms of life, other experiences, and the voyage and the exploration, the delving into character, the vast expanse of life's possibilities, contemplation of future travels, of dazzling friendships, all this then makes the chores and the sacrifices beautiful because they are diverted toward some beautiful aim, they become part of the structure of a work of art.

—Diary 5, pp. 130-131

· 292 ·

In our dreams and in our fantasies we are all surrealists, impressionists, abstractionists, symbolists.

—Diary 5, pg. 136

· 293 ·

I believe one writes because one has to create a world in which one can live. I could not live in any of the worlds offered to me—the world of my parents, the world of Henry Miller, the world of Gonzalo, or the world of wars. I had to create a world of my own, like a climate, a country, an atmosphere in which I could breathe, reign, and re-create myself when destroyed by living. That, I believe, is the reason for every work of art.

—Diary 5, pg. 149

· 294 ·

The artist is the only one who knows that the world is a subjective creation, that there is a choice to be made, a selection of elements. It is a materialization, an incarnation of his inner world. Then he hopes to attract others into it. He hopes to impose his particular vision and share it with others. And when the second stage is not reached, the brave artist continues nevertheless. The few moments of communion with the world are worth the pain, for it is a world for others, an inheritance for others, a gift to others, in the end.

—Diary 5, pg. 149

· 295 ·

We…write to heighten our own awareness of life. We write to lure and enchant and console others. We write to serenade our lovers.

—Diary 5, pg. 149

· 296 ·

We write to taste life twice, in the moment, and
in retrospection.

—Diary 5, pg. 149

· 297 ·

We write, like Proust, to render all of it eternal, and to
persuade ourselves that it is eternal.

—Diary 5, pp. 149-150

· 298 ·

We write to be able to transcend our life, to reach
beyond it.

—Diary 5, pg. 150

· 299 ·

We write to teach ourselves to speak with others, to record
the journey into the labyrinth.

—Diary 5, pg. 150

· 300 ·

We write to expand our world when we feel strangled, or
constricted, or lonely.

—Diary 5, pg. 150

· 301 ·

We write as the birds sing, as the primitives dance their rituals.

—Diary 5, pg. 150

· 302 ·

If you do not breathe through writing, if you do not cry out in writing, or sing in writing, then don't write, because our culture has no use for it.

—Diary 5, pg. 150

· 303 ·

When I don't write, I feel my world shrinking. I feel I am in a prison. I feel I lose my fire and my color. It should be a necessity, as the sea needs to heave, and I call it breathing.

—Diary 5, pg. 150

· 304 ·

The role of the writer is not to say what we can all say, but what we are unable to say.

—Diary 5, pg. 171

Writing and Art

· 305 ·

The writer's responsibility is to increase, develop our senses, expand our vision, heighten our awareness and enrich our articulateness.

—Diary 5, pg. 171

· 306 ·

The common man neither feels nor thinks as he talks. He has not learned to talk. And that is our role, to talk for him, exactly as the virtuoso violinist plays for him a violin he cannot play.

—Diary 5, pg. 191

· 307 ·

What people really fight in the artist is his freedom, his attempts at freeing himself from human bondage. He forfeits and repudiates his human family if they seek to enslave him to a profession or a religion he does not believe in. He pays the price with solitude.

—Diary 5, pg. 192

· 308 ·

In my work I meant to begin in the subconscious and arrive at objectivity. I intended to unite them.

—Diary 5, pg. 235

· 309 ·

The poet lives in a transfigured night—the night of symbols. Even when he mentions the dreams and interweaves them, he reveals very little of the blind unconscious pattern and compulsions they betray.

—Diary 6, pg. 26

· 310 ·

It was…dangerous to dig for coal, gold, oil, yet men were willing to lose their lives for it. The writer dares to dig into hidden worlds, dares perilous explorations in which he might lose, first of all, his contact with human life and possibly his sanity. But he is looking for treasures of another kind.

—Diary 6, pg. 35

· 311 ·

The reason the writer must not translate symbolic images is that we must all learn the language of symbolism. Otherwise we will never become familiar with it and we need to know it to interpret our daily acts… It is the language of our hidden self.

—Diary 6, pg. 47

· 312 ·

Among a thousand other things, I ask myself if it is possible to find completeness in human companionship. In contemplating love, I foresaw the abandonment of my diary. In fulfilling love, I still cling tenaciously to these pages. The reason I need you is to receive the emotions and ideas which overflow from my being.

—Early Diary 2, pg. 6

· 313 ·

Jesting, I begged Hugo to break me of the vice of diary writing. He objected. It was rather a privilege to be endowed with the habit of writing.

—Early Diary 2, pg. 7

· 314 ·

I am caught in a circle. At first I wished only to exercise, to develop, to attain ease and fluency, but now I cannot cease.

—Early Diary 2, pg. 7

· 315 ·

To willfully ignore sorrow, to guide the thoughts into detached channels—that is the acme of mental weakness, and yet sometimes the result of unbearable pressure. To steady myself, to retain my evenness, I sometimes avoid the subjects closest to me.

—Early Diary 2, pg. 7

· 316 ·

Dearest diary, you are the living symbol of my failure, as the world sees failure, but you are the representative of all I hold sacred, which is the subtle transition of thoughts and emotions into words, which are to me invested with the holiest of joys.

—Early Diary 2, pp. 7-8

· 317 ·

Some, if my writing reached them, this writing that I have done walking alone, would know that there are several of us walking alone…

—Early Diary 4, pg. 25

· 318 ·

In creation alone there is the possibility of perfection.

—Fire, pg. 86

· 319 ·

Creation which cannot express itself becomes madness.

—Fire, pg. 321

· 320 ·

I really believe that if I were not a writer, not a creator, not an experimenter, I might have been a very faithful wife.

—Henry & June, pg. 12

Writing and Art

· 321 ·

I think highly of faithfulness. But my temperament belongs to the writer, not to the woman.

—*Henry & June*, pg. 12

· 322 ·

Writers make love to whatever they need.

—*Henry & June*, pg. 54

· 323 ·

I speak of relief when I write; perhaps, but it is also an engraving of pain, a tattooing of myself.

—*Henry & June*, pg. 207

· 324 ·

This abdication of life demanded of the artist is to be achieved only relatively. Most artists have *retired* too absolutely; they grow rusty, inflexible to the flow of currents.

—*Incest*, pg. 46

· 325 ·

I realize that the diary is a struggle to seize upon the most unseizable person on earth. I elude my own detection.

—*Incest*, pg. 141

· 326 ·

Every day I must say, "Courage, *audace*, maturity, face life, face the public as woman, as artist. Harden. Toughen. Toughen."

—Incest, pg. 141

· 327 ·

I remember minutely certain things which torment me until I have set them down. When I have written a thing I no longer fear the loss of it. It is an insane love of life, of human life.

—Incest, pg. 241

· 328 ·

I need a place where I can shout and weep. I have to be a Spanish savage at some time of the day. I record here the hysteria life causes in me. The overflow of an undisciplined extravagance. To hell with taste and art, with all contractions and polishings. Here I shout, I dance, I weep, I gnash my teeth, I go mad—all by myself, in bad English, in chaos. It will keep me sane for the world and for art.

—Incest, pg. 280

· 329 ·

I don't care about the pain… I think only of the book I will write.

—Incest, pg. 314

· 330 ·

Instead of writing a book, I lie back and talk to myself. A drug. I turn away from reality into the refracted, I turn events into vapor, into languid dreams.

—Incest, pg. 366

· 331 ·

Covering all things with the mist of smoke, deforming and transforming as the night does. All matter must be fused this way for me through the lens of my vice, or the rust of living would slow down my rhythm to a sob.

—Incest, pg. 366

· 332 ·

My definition of art is an act of human love.

—Incest, pg. 369

· 333 ·

Psychoanalysis did save me, because it allowed the birth of the real me, who is religious. I may not become a saint. But I am very full and very rich, and I have a great deal to write about.

—Incest, pg. 403

· 334 ·

By the beginning of the diary, I was already conceding that life would be more bearable if I looked at it as an adventure and a tale. I was telling myself the story of my life, and this transmutes into an adventure the things which can shatter you.

—Preface to *Linotte*, page vii

· 335 ·

These last days I have written many stories. Then when I am tired I sit at the window which looks out on the ugly courtyard, but as a consolation I imagine that it's a countryside. I pretend the ugly dry plants are beautiful flowers, the ugly red wall a beautiful golden gate that is the entrance to the grounds of a pretty chateau. Then once I am inside I think endlessly, I imagine that the Negro servants are handsome little princes who walk about in their chateau. Perhaps those are foolish ideas, but they are true and perhaps I am mad. So much the worse for me. I like being like that and I shall always be that way, for I have no intention of changing until someone more sensible than I tells me to, and even then it will be with regret.

—*Linotte*, pg. 30, age 11

· 336 ·

Write. It is your ornament, your grace, your seduction, your chant for courting.

—*Mirages*, pg. 30

· 337 ·

I cannot go into new lives without my books. They
are my boat and sail, my passport and map, my compass
and telescope.

—*Mirages*, pg. 92

· 338 ·

Listen to me, you English readers! I am sacrificing myself
for you. I left my own people—those who *understand* my
language. I left them to bring you the subtle melodies, the
infinite nuances. In doing so, I seek difficulties, I shall be
often rejected. You deal in terrible simplicities, in deserts,
in primitive in-differentiation. You lack overtones. You
lack the oblique, the indirect, the range, the virtuosity
and maturity. Listen to me! I am your most intricate and
variable musician. I can extend your ears, add hundreds of
colors to your eyes, increase your palate's responsiveness,
develop your senses. Follow me! I am bringing you a
gift. As eyes, you are colorblind. My blood itself, my
race brings you color. You lack tonalities. If you would
accustom your ears to my scales, to my great variations,
wavelengths, how light you would grow, what worlds you
would discover! I could make you sensitive all over, thin
your skin, sensitize your senses—if you let me! Are you
going to punish me for my audacity? The awakener! Proust
has not penetrated you. You cannot read Giraudoux. But I
speak *your* language—the language of the potential you.

—*Mirages*, pg. 147

· 339 ·

The truth, which only the child and the artist tell, is the real wonder. Magic and power lie in the truth, the truth.

—*Mirages*, pg. 335

· 340 ·

It is the function of art to renew our perception. What we are familiar with we cease to see. The writer shakes up the familiar scene, and as if by magic, we see a new meaning in it.

—*The Novel of the Future*, pg. 25

· 341 ·

It is when we use will and force to impose an artificial structure that we become sterile.

—*The Novel of the Future*, pg. 29

· 342 ·

The writing of a novel is, in a sense, a directed dream, embroidered upon a certain theme of thought or sensation.

—*The Novel of the Future*, pg. 32

· 343 ·

To write without feeling is to miss the one element which animates every line.

—*The Novel of the Future*, pg. 55

· 344 ·

The closer a writer keeps to emotional reality, the more alive the writing will be.

—The Novel of the Future, pg. 83

· 345 ·

The writer's role is express what we cannot express. He is our virtuoso; he can help us out of our prison of inarticulateness.

—The Novel of the Future, pg. 91

· 346 ·

Someone told Shakespeare: "That is not the way people talk." Shakespeare answered: "No, but that is the way they should talk."

—The Novel of the Future, pg. 99

· 347 ·

There still remains to be achieved the enormous task of convincing man that poetic language is…the only expression we have for the complexities and subtleties of our emotions and perceptions as we know from the study of our dreams.

—The Novel of the Future, pg. 101

· 348 ·

The mood of a book is like the personality of a human being. It draws to itself what belongs to it.

—Novel of the Future, pg. 128

· 349 ·

The writer who should be our guide fails when he sees each person only from the outside as a statue.

—The Novel of the Future, pg. 132

· 350 ·

Writing every day as one practices the piano every day keeps one nimble, and then when the great moments of inspiration come, one is in good form, supple and smooth.

—The Novel of the Future, pg. 146

· 351 ·

Henry Miller was never concerned with the faithfulness of his descriptions. He was not concerned with resemblance at all. He invented a world of his own, personages of his own, including himself.

—The Novel of the Future, pg. 156

Writing and Art

· 352 ·

The preoccupation of the novelist: how to capture the living moment… You write while they are alive. You do not preserve them in alcohol until the moment you are ready to write about them.

—*The Novel of the Future*, pg. 160

· 353 ·

For me the act of rewriting was tampering with the freshness and aliveness. I preferred to cut.

—*The Novel of the Future*, pg. 162

· 354 ·

Everything can nourish the writer. The dictionary, a new word, a voyage, an encounter, a talk in the street, a book, a phrase heard. He is a computer set to receive and utilize all things. An exhibit of painting, a concert, a voice, a letter, a play, a landscape, a skyscape, a telephone conversation, a nap, a dream, a sleepless night, a storm, an animal's greeting, an aquarium, a photograph, a newspaper story.

—*The Novel of the Future*, pg. 164

· 355 ·

The function of a novel is to give you an emotional experience.

—*The Novel of the Future*, pg. 168

· 356 ·

The creative writer is the one who teaches expansion and liberation of the human mind.

—*The Novel of the Future*, pg. 169

· 357 ·

Experiment and research in the novel are just as necessary as they are in art or science. They break old molds which can no longer express new visions.

—*The Novel of the Future*, pg. 195

· 358 ·

What art gives us, and the near and individual document does not, is the vision of all that lies beyond the personal, which makes the personal, the human, bearable.

—*Trapeze*, pg. 238

· 361 ·

I have only been able to bear the cruelties and abominations of human life by transfigurations: art, poetry, fantasy.

—*Trapeze*, pg. 330

· 359 ·

The hell traversed by the artist most human beings are unwilling to traverse.

—*Trapeze*, pg. 357

· 360 ·

The artist submits himself to adventures into the irrational. He is merely another type of adventurer.

—Trapeze, pg. 357

· 362 ·

I feel like a minor Einstein, a mathematician of the emotions whom only a few can read.

—unpublished diary, 1955

· 363 ·

When someone is wounded, first sympathy, then first aid, then combat negativity with creativity.

—unpublished diary, 1955

· 364 ·

Music melts all the separate parts of our bodies together.

—The Winter of Artifice (1939 edition), pg. 164

· 365 ·

Great art was born of great terror, great loneliness, great inhibitions, instabilities, and it always balances them.

—A Woman Speaks, pg. 5

380

I am inserting into
English writing the
subtlety and multi-
lateral aspects it
lacks. The language
obeys me. But it will
be difficult to be
heard, seen, touched
and loved by the
English palate and
soul. Listen to me,
you English readers!
I am sacrificing
myself for you. I
left my own people —
those who understand
my language — I
left them to bring you

the subtle melodies,
the infinite nuances –
In doing so, I such
difficulties, I shall be
often rejected. You deal
in terrible simplicities,
in deserts, in premature
undifferenciations. You
lack overtones – You
lack the oblique, the
indirect, the range, the
virtuosity and maturity.
Listen to me! I am your
most intricate and
variable musician. I
can extend your ears
add hundred colors to
your eyes, increase your
palate's responsiveness –
develop your senses –
follow me!

ABOUT THE AUTHOR:
A CHRONOLOGY

1903   Anaïs Nin born in Neuilly, France

1913   Nin's father abandons family

1914   Nin, her mother and two brothers come to New York;
       begins her diary, in French

1920   Begins to write her diary in English

1923   Marries Hugh P. Guiler, a banker, in Cuba

1924   Nin and Guiler move to Paris; Nin continues her diary
       and dabbles in fiction

1931   Meets controversial American novelist Henry Miller in
       Louveciennes, France

1932   Becomes Miller's lover and is infatuated with his wife
       June; Edward Titus publishes Nin's *D. H. Lawrence: An
       Unprofessional Study*

1933   Reunites with her father and they begin an
       incestuous relationship

1934   Comes to New York to help Otto Rank psychoanalyze patients;
       becomes Rank's lover

1936   Self-publishes *The House of Incest* (Siana Editions); meets
       Gonalo Moré

1937   Meets Lawrence Durrell; she, Miller and Durrell begin planning
       a series of books

1939   Obelisk Press prints Nin's *The Winter of Artifice*; Nin
       and Guiler fly to New York to avoid oncoming war

1940   Reunites with her two lovers, Miller and Moré, in New York

1942   Self-publishes *Winter of Artifice* (Gemor Press); breaks
       with Miller

1944   Self-publishes *Under a Glass Bell* (Gemor Press)

1945   Self-publishes *This Hunger* (Gemor Press); meets Gore Vidal

1946   E. P. Dutton publishes *Ladders to Fire*

1947   Dutton publishes *Children of the Albatross*; Nin meets Rupert Pole and drives to California with him; begins her "double life," dividing her time between Pole in California and Guiler in New York; breaks with Moré

1950   Duell, Sloan and Pearce publishes *The Four-Chambered Heart*

1954   The British Book Centre publishes *A Spy in the House of Love*

1955   Nin bigamously marries Pole

1957   Avon republishes *A Spy in the House of Love*, which becomes Nin's best seller to date

1958   Self-publishes *Solar Barque*

1959   Self-publishes *Cities of the Interior*

1961   Signs with publisher Alan Swallow, who publishes *Seduction of the Minotaur* and reprints her earlier fiction

1964   Swallow publishes *Collages*, Nin's final work of fiction

1966   Harcourt Brace Jovanovich/Swallow publish volume one of *The Diary of Anaïs Nin*; Nin becomes famous and begins a popular lecture tour that would last for years

1967   Volume 2 of the *Diary* is published

1968   Swallow publishes *The Novel of the Future*

1969   Volume 3 of the *Diary* is published

1971   Volume 4 of the *Diary* is published

1974   Volume 5 of the *Diary* is published; Nin learns she has cancer

1975   Nin's health deteriorates; remains in Los Angeles with Pole

1976   Volume 6 of the *Diary* is published; Nin is named Woman of the Year by the *Los Angeles Times*

1977   Nin dies at 73; *Delta of Venus* is published posthumously and becomes her best seller

WORKS CITED

Cities of the Interior (*Ladders to Fire, Children of the Albatross, The Four-Chambered Heart, A Spy in the House of Love, Seduction of the Minotaur*). San Antonio: Sky Blue Press, 2013. Digital. Athens, OH: Swallow Press, 1974. Print.

Collages. San Antonio: Sky Blue Press, 2010. Digital. Athens, OH: Swallow Press, 1964. Print.

D. H. Lawrence: An Unprofessional Study. San Antonio: Sky Blue Press, 2011. Digital. Athens, OH: Swallow Press, 1964. Print.

Delta of Venus: Erotica. New York: Harcourt Brace Jovanovich, 1977. Print. Digital.

The Diary of Anaïs Nin, Volume 1, 1931-1934. New York: Harcourt Brace Jovanovich, 1966. Print. Digital. Referenced as *Diary 1*.

The Diary of Anaïs Nin, Volume 2, 1934-1939. New York: Harcourt Brace & World, Inc., 1967. Print. Digital. Referenced as *Diary 2*.

The Diary of Anaïs Nin, Volume 3, 1939-1944. New York: Harcourt Brace Jovanovich, 1969. Print. Digital. Referenced as *Diary 3*.

The Diary of Anaïs Nin, Volume 4, 1944-1947. New York: Harcourt Brace Jovanovich, 1971. Print. Digital. Referenced as *Diary 4*.

The Diary of Anaïs Nin, Volume 5, 1947-1955. New York: Harcourt Brace Jovanovich, 1974. Print. Digital. Referenced as *Diary 5*.

The Diary of Anaïs Nin, Volume 6, 1955-1966. New York: Harcourt Brace Jovanovich. 1976. Print. Digital. Referenced as *Diary 6*.

The Diary of Anaïs Nin, Volume 7, 1966-1974. New York: Harcourt Brace Jovanovich, 1980. Print. Referenced as *Diary 7*.

Linotte: The Early Diary of Anaïs Nin, 1914-1920. New York: Harcourt Brace Jovanovich, 1978. Print. Referenced as *Linotte*.

The Early Diary of Anaïs Nin, Volume 2, 1920-1923. New York: Harcourt Brace Jovanovich, 1982. Print. Referenced as *Early Diary 2*.

The Early Diary of Anaïs Nin, Volume 4, 1927-1931. New York: Harcourt Brace Jovanovich, 1985. Print. References as *Early Diary 4*.

Fire: From "A Journal of Love," The Unexpurgated Diary of Anaïs Nin, 1933-1937. New York: Harcourt Brace, 1995. Print. Digital. Referenced as *Fire.*

Henry & June: From the Unexpurgated Diary of Anaïs Nin. New York: Harcourt Brace Jovanovich, 1986. Print. Referenced as *Henry & June.*

House of Incest. San Antonio: Sky Blue Press, 2010. Digital. Athens, OH: Swallow Press, 1995. Print.

In Favor of the Sensitive Man and Other Essays. New York: Harcourt Brace Jovanovich, 1976. Print. Digital. Referenced as *In Favor of the Sensitive Man.*

Incest: From "A Journal of Love," The Unexpurgated Diary of Anaïs Nin, 1932-1933. New York: Harcourt Brace Jovanovich, 1992. Print. Digital. Referenced as *Incest.*

Mirages: The Unexpurgated Diary of Anaïs Nin, 1939-1947. San Antonio: Sky Blue Press, 2013. Digital. Athens, OH: Swallow Press/Sky Blue Press, 2013. Print. Referenced as *Mirages.*

The Novel of the Future. San Antonio: Sky Blue Press, 2014. Digital. Athens, OH: Swallow Press, 1968. Print.

Trapeze: The Unexpurgated Diary of Anaïs Nin, 1947-1955. San Antonio: Sky Blue Press, 2016. Print and digital. Referenced as *Trapeze.*

Under a Glass Bell. San Antonio: Sky Blue Press, 2010. Digital. Athens, OH: Swallow Press, 2014. Print.

The Winter of Artifice: 1939 Paris Edition. San Antonio: Sky Blue Press, 2007. Print; 2009. Digital.

Winter of Artifice (American edition). San Antonio: Sky Blue Press (digital publication pending). Athens, OH: Swallow Press, 1961. Print.

A Woman Speaks. San Antonio: Sky Blue Press (digital publication pending). Athens, OH: Swallow Press, 1975. Print.

PERMISSIONS INFORMATION

ALSO AVAILABLE FROM
SKY BLUE PRESS

Trapeze: The Unexpurgated Diary of Anaïs Nin, 1947-1955
by Anaïs Nin. (print, ebook) ... Coming in 2016

Mirages: The Unexpurgated Diary of Anaïs Nin, 1939-1947
by Anaïs Nin (ebook)

The Portable Anaïs Nin by Anaïs Nin, ed. Benjamin Franklin V
(print, ebook)

D.H. Lawrence: An Unprofessional Study by Anaïs Nin (ebook)

House of Incest by Anaïs Nin (ebook)

The Winter of Artifice: 1939 Paris Edition by Anaïs Nin
(print, ebook)

Under a Glass Bell by Anaïs Nin (ebook)

Stella by Anaïs Nin (ebook)

Ladders to Fire by Anaïs Nin (ebook)

Children of the Albatross by Anaïs Nin (ebook)

The Four-Chambered Heart by Anaïs Nin (ebook)

A Spy in the House of Love by Anaïs Nin (ebook)

Seduction of the Minotaur by Anaïs Nin (ebook)

Cities of the Interior by Anaïs Nin (ebook)

Collages by Anaïs Nin (ebook)

The Novel of the Future by Anaïs Nin (ebook)

Anaïs Nin: The Last Days, a Memoir by Barbara Kraft (ebook)

Anaïs Nin's Lost World: Paris in Words and Pictures 1924-1939
by Britt Arenander (ebook)

Anaïs Nin Character Dictionary and Index to Diary Excerpts by Benjamin Franklin V (print, ebook)

A Café in Space: The Anaïs Nin Literary Journal, Vol. 1 by Anaïs Nin, Janet Fitch, Lynette Felber (print, ebook)

A Café in Space: The Anaïs Nin Literary Journal, Vol. 2 by Anaïs Nin, Benjamin Franklin V, Masako Meio... (print, ebook)

A Café in Space: The Anaïs Nin Literary Journal, Vol. 3 by Anaïs Nin, Gunther Stuhlmann, Richard Pine, James Clawson... (print, ebook)

A Café in Space: The Anaïs Nin Literary Journal, Vol. 4 by Anaïs Nin, Alan Swallow, John Ferrone, Yuko Yaguchi...
(print, ebook)

A Café in Space: The Anaïs Nin Literary Journal, Vol. 5 by Anaïs Nin, Duane Schneider, Sarah Burghauser... (print, ebook)

A Café in Space: The Anaïs Nin Literary Journal, Vol. 6 by Anaïs Nin, Joaquín Nin y Castellanos, Tristine Rainer, Christie Logan... (print, ebook)

A Café in Space: The Anaïs Nin Literary Journal, Vol. 7 by Anaïs Nin, John Ferrone, Kim Krizan, Tristine Rainer...

A Café in Space: The Anaïs Nin Literary Journal, Vol. 8 by Anaïs Nin, Benjamin Franklin V, Anita Jarczok, Kim Krizan... (print, ebook)

A Café in Space: The Anaïs Nin Literary Journal, Vol. 9 by Anaïs Nin, Anita Jarczok, Joel Enos... (print, ebook)

A Café in Space: The Anaïs Nin Literary Journal, Vol. 10 by Anaïs Nin, Benjamin Franklin V, Kim Krizan, William Claire, Erin Dunbar...
(print, ebook)

A Café in Space: The Anaïs Nin Literary Journal, Vol. 11 by Anaïs Nin, Henry Miller, Alfred Perlès, John Tytell (print, ebook)

A Café in Space: The Anaïs Nin Literary Journal, Vol. 12 by Anaïs Nin, Kim Krizan, Benjamin Franklin V (print, ebook)

A SELECTED LIST OF PRINT WORKS
ABOUT ANAÏS NIN

ANAIS: An International Journal, ed. Gunther Stuhlmann
—Anaïs Nin Foundation

Anaïs Nin's Narratives, ed. Anne T. Salvatore
—University Press of Florida

A Café in Space: The Anaïs Nin Literary Journal, ed. Paul Herron
—Sky Blue Press

Barbara Kraft, *Anaïs Nin: The Last Days*
—Sky Blue Press; Pegasus Books

Benjamin Franklin V, *Anaïs Nin Character Dictionary and Index to Diary Excerpts*—Sky Blue Press

Suzanne Nalbantian, *Aesthetic Autobiography: From Life to Art in Marcel Proust, James Joyce, Virginia Woolf, and Anaïs Nin*
—Palgrave Macmillan

Recollections of Anaïs Nin by her Contemporaries, ed.
Benjamin Franklin V—Ohio University Press

Diane Richard-Allerdyce, *Anaïs Nin and the Remaking of Self: Gender, Modernism, and Narrative Identity*—Northern Illinois University Press

A SELECTED LIST OF PRINT WORKS BY ANAÏS NIN

D. H. Lawrence: An Unprofessional Study
—Swallow/Ohio University (OU) Press

House of Incest—Swallow/OU Press

The Winter of Artifice (original edition)—Sky Blue Press

Winter of Artifice (revised edition)—Swallow/OU Press

Under a Glass Bell—Swallow/OU Press

Cities of the Interior (consisting of 5 novels)—Swallow/OU Press

Ladders to Fire

Children of the Albatross

The Four-Chambered Heart

A Spy in the House of Love

Seduction of the Minotaur

Collages—Swallow/OU Press

The Novel of the Future—Swallow/OU Press

The Diary of Anaïs Nin (7 volumes)—Houghton Mifflin Harcourt (HMH)

The Early Diary of Anaïs Nin (4 volumes)—HMH

Henry and June: From the Unexpurgated Diary of Anaïs Nin—HMH

Incest: From "A Journal of Love"—HMH

Fire: From "A Journal of Love"—HMH

Nearer the Moon: From "A Journal of Love"—HMH

Mirages: The Unexpurgated Diary of Anaïs Nin
—Swallow/OU Press/Sky Blue Press

Delta of Venus—HMH

Little Birds—HMH

ANAÏS NIN ONLINE

Anaïs Nin Blog
http://anaisninblog.skybluepress.com

Anaïs Nin Podcast
iTunes:
https://itunes.apple.com/us/podcast/anais-nin/id969808038?mt=2
or
http://anaisninblog.skybluepress.com/category/anais-nin-podcast/

Anaïs Nin on Twitter
@anaisninblog

Sky Blue Press and Anaïs Nin on Pinterest
www.pinterest.com/skybluepress/

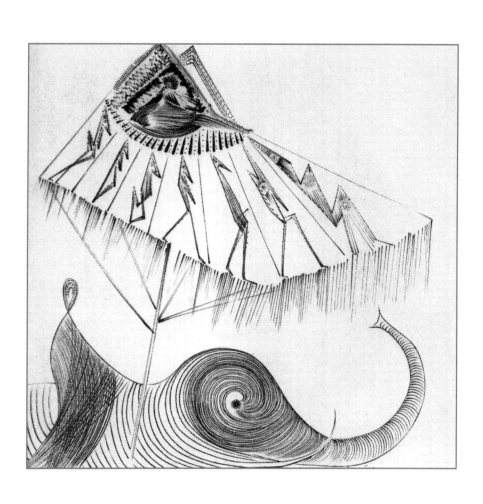

Printed in Great Britain
by Amazon

43808339R00072